THE WORLD IS ROUND

Also by Anthony Ravielli

Wonders of the Human Body
An Adventure in Geometry

THE WORLD

S ROUND

WRITTEN AND ILLUSTRATED BY

ANTHONY RAVIELLI

NEW YORK · THE VIKING PRESS

Printed in the U.S.A.

To Jane, Ellen, and Tony, Jr.

Who help make the world go round

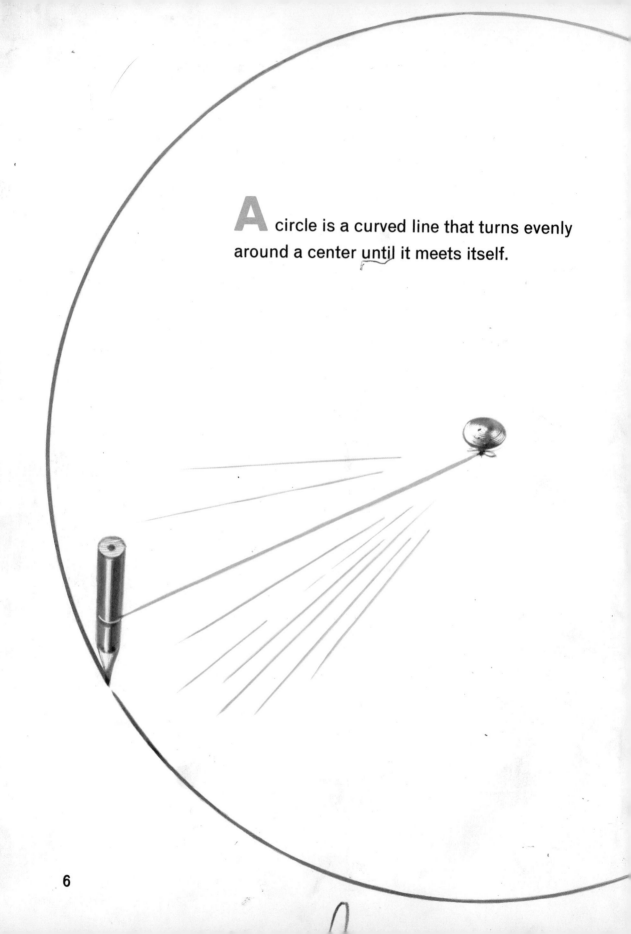

A circle is a curved line that turns evenly around a center until it meets itself.

6

The edge of a penny is a circle.

If you spin a penny,

its edge, as it turns, blurs to look like a perfectly round ball.

A perfectly round ball is called a sphere. Its outer edge, or circumference, always looks like a circle no matter how you turn it.

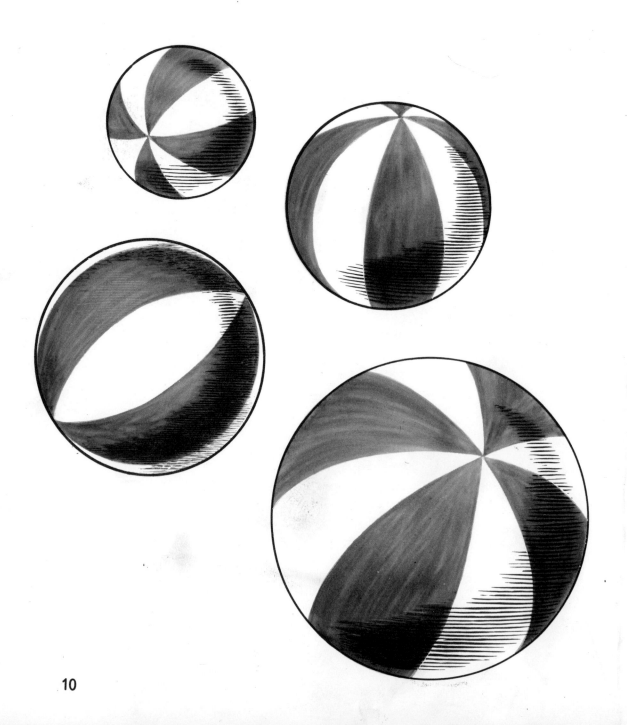

If you close your eyes and hold a ball in your hands, its shape always feels the same, no matter what part of the ball you touch.

A sphere looks like a ball only if it is small enough for us to see its entire circumference at one time.

But a fly landing on a ball would see only part of the surface. The edge of the ball the fly sees at any one time is only a portion of a circle.

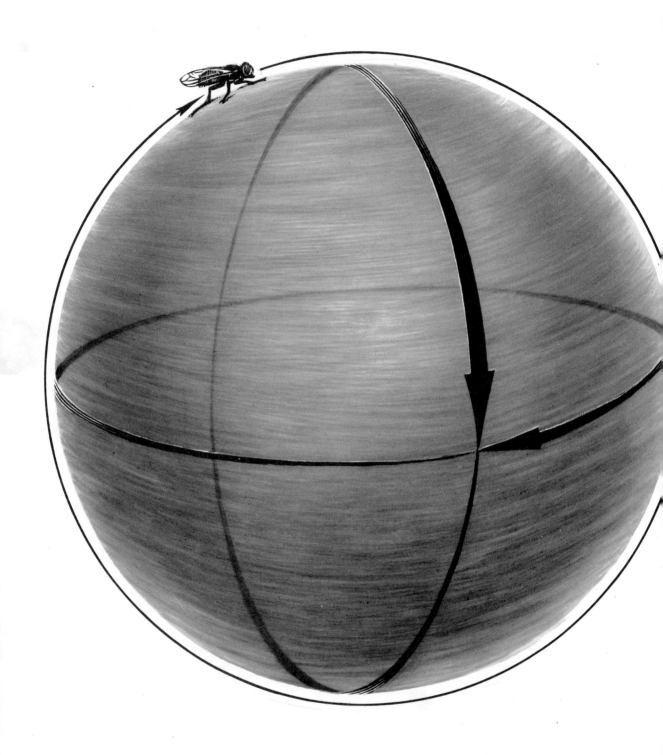

When the fly is on the ball, the spot it stands on may feel like a curved surface, but what the fly sees does not look like a ball. If the fly were as clever as we are, it could easily discover it was on a ball because, if it walked straight ahead in any one direction, the fly would soon return to the exact spot from which it started.

Now imagine a ball the size of a house.

To a fly standing on this giant ball the tiny piece of the circumference it sees would hardly seem to curve. And the part of the ball
the fly stands on would be such a tiny portion of the surface that
to the fly (even a clever fly) it would seem to be flat.

The world we live on is a giant ball spinning through space.

18

It is so big that its horizon, the edge of the world where the sky meets the

earth, even when seen from a jet plane ten miles high, seems to be flat.

We are so tiny compared to the gigantic ball we live on that we see only a speck of its surface. That part of the world we do see does not look like a portion of a ball. The surfaces of calm seas and of lakes and rivers look flat to us. And the land, rough and uneven, spreads around us like a lumpy carpet. In fact, we live our lives and build our bridges and houses as though the world were flat.

Until a few hundred years ago most people actually believed the world was a gigantic disk—flat as a pancake. In their imagination the land they lived on was in the center of the disk, and surrounding the land was the sea.

The sea (they thought) extended to the very edge of their flat
world. They were absolutely sure that if a ship sailed too far away
from land it would topple over the edge of the world into the no-
where of empty space.

But throughout the ages there have always been a few wise men who looked at the world around them with inquiring eyes.

In ancient Greece, scholars studied the sky when the nights were clear. They noted the changing shape of the moon, the wanderings of the planets, and the patterns formed by the stars. They wondered if our world was a part of the splendor they saw in the sky.

The idea that the surface of the world is curved is about twenty-five hundred years old. The early Greeks were the first to suspect it as they noticed changes in the starry skies when they traveled south to Egypt. They saw new stars in the night sky and could no longer see some familiar ones. Stars that sparkled low over the southern horizon in Egypt, for example, could not be seen at all in the sky over Greece, five hundred miles to the north. If the earth were flat, the night sky would always contain the same stars. These changes in the skies could be explained only if the surface of the earth was curved. But some scholars thought it curved in only one direction —north to south.

A famous Greek scholar named Pythagoras, who lived more than five hundred years before the birth of Christ, probably was the first to declare that the earth is a sphere. Perhaps he was gazing at the open sea from a hilltop and noticed that ships, as they sailed away in any direction, disappeared gradually over the horizon. The hull always vanished first, then the sail, until only the top of the mast could be seen; and, finally, there was no trace—as if the ship had been swallowed by the sea. When a ship returned, the top of the mast reappeared first, then more and more of the sail became visible, and then the entire ship loomed into view.

From such observations Pythagoras may have realized that the earth, like a sphere, is curved in all directions. But his idea was believed only by his own followers, who handed his teachings down from one generation to the next.

Then, two hundred years later, the great Greek scholar Aristotle saw something in the sky that proved Pythagoras was right—the earth is a sphere.

Like the earth, the moon has no light of its own. It shines by reflecting the light of the sun. During the moon's monthly journey around the earth, a varying portion of its sunlit surface is visible from the earth. Once a month in the night sky, when the moon and the sun are on opposite sides of the earth, the moon is full—its entire face is bright with sunlight. Usually, the full moon travels above or below the shadow cast by the earth. But sometimes the earth's shadow is directly in the path of the moon. Then the full moon darkens as it passes into the shadow. This event is called an eclipse of the moon.

Aristotle, while watching an eclipse of the moon, noticed the shape of the shadow that spread slowly over the moon's face. He saw that the earth's shadow was circular—like the shadow cast by a sphere.

To Aristotle and his followers such evidence was enough to prove that the world was round. There was no need for them, like our imaginary fly, to circle the globe to know they were on a ball. In fact, with only the few clues they had and the aid of mathematics, some Greek scholars were able to figure out the size of this gigantic ball. Although their figures for the size were not exactly right, these men knew the world was just too big for anyone on earth to see even a small part of its curve.

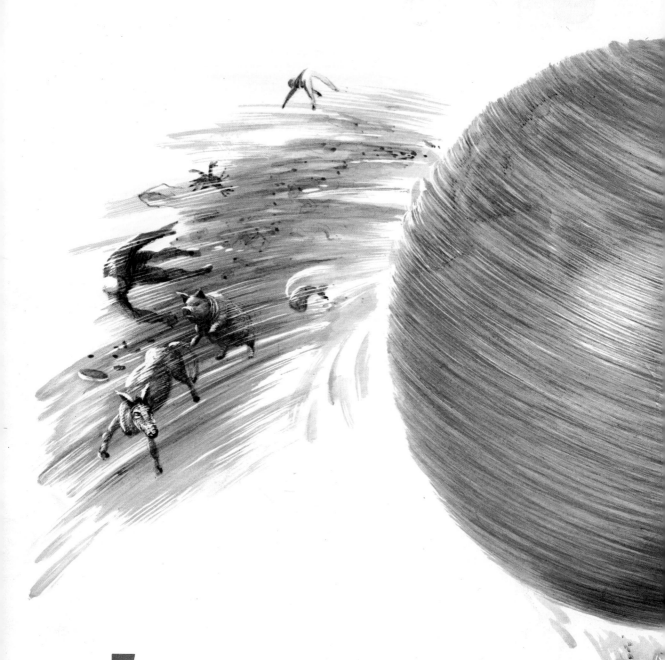

E ven in ancient times, however, and for hundreds of years there-
after, only a handful of men were convinced that the earth is a globe
spinning around its own axis. The rest of the people clung to the
belief that the earth was flat. To them, the idea of a round earth

made no sense at all. If the earth is a ball, they said, whatever is on the other side of the world would be upside down and would fall off. And if this ball is spinning, all of us would be flung into space. They did not know about the force of gravity, which pulls everything toward the center of the earth—even the air and the clouds.

Although the belief that the world is round was recorded in books, most people could neither read nor write and cared little for ideas about the shape of the world. Even those bold navigators of the past, the Vikings, did not seem to be concerned about such things. They left no records that tell us whether they thought the world was round or flat. As far as we know, they were simply reckless adventurers who sailed the seas without fear. They went wherever the winds carried their strange, sturdy open boats and are believed even to have crossed the Atlantic Ocean in search of lands to plunder. To the other peoples of Europe, however, the oceans were fearful, unknown waters because until the fifteenth century, two thousand years after Pythagoras, almost everybody still believed the earth was flat.

About five hundred years ago, Christopher Columbus, a navigator who studied the books of the wise men, took the first giant step that led to the final proof that the world is round. Columbus, by putting into action ideas that had been known to scholars for centuries, ended forever the image of a flat world.

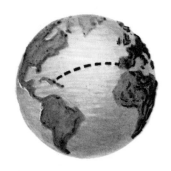

All of us have heard the story of Christopher Columbus—how, in 1492, with three tiny ships and a crew of men who thought they were doomed, he set sail for India on a course that no one before him had ever taken. After sailing for seventy-one days, he landed on the shores of an island near a continent he never knew existed. Columbus thought he had circled the globe and had reached India. We know he hadn't. But he did open the door to a new world, and he paved the way for Magellan's attempt, in 1519, to circumnavigate the globe. Three years later, although Magellan had been killed in the Philippine Islands, one of his ships completed the voyage. It was the first time man had ever traveled completely around the world.

Since the days of Columbus men have gone around the world in all directions. At first, the trip was a dangerous adventure that took years. Now, anyone can go around the world in days. Astronauts do it in minutes. Whether it takes years, days, or minutes, we know that if we, like the fly on a ball, move along a proper course in a fixed direction, we will return to the same place from which we started. That is all the proof we need to tell us we are on a sphere.

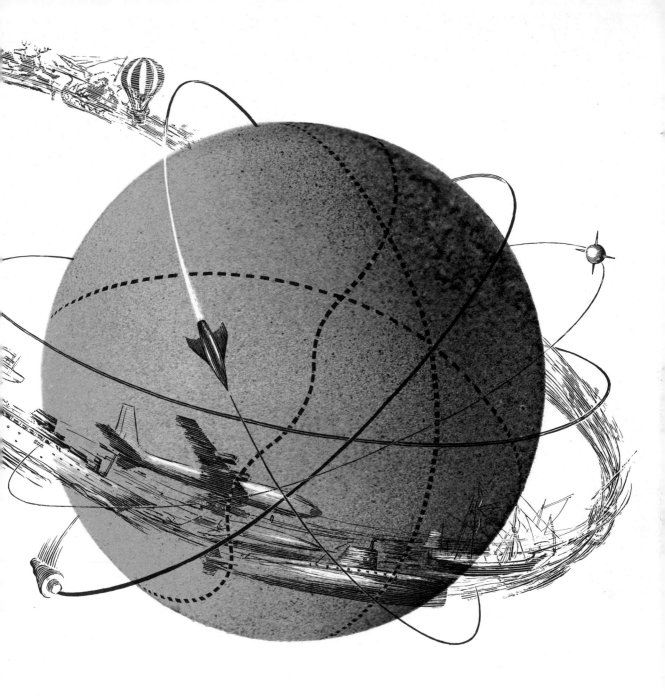

Even though we take it for granted that the world is round, no one, since the beginning of time, has ever seen the world as a ball. It is so big that even astronauts, hundreds of miles out in space, see only a small portion of the sphere at a time. Only from thousands of miles away can a globe the size of our world be seen as a whole.

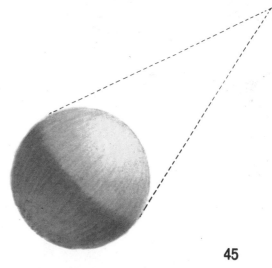

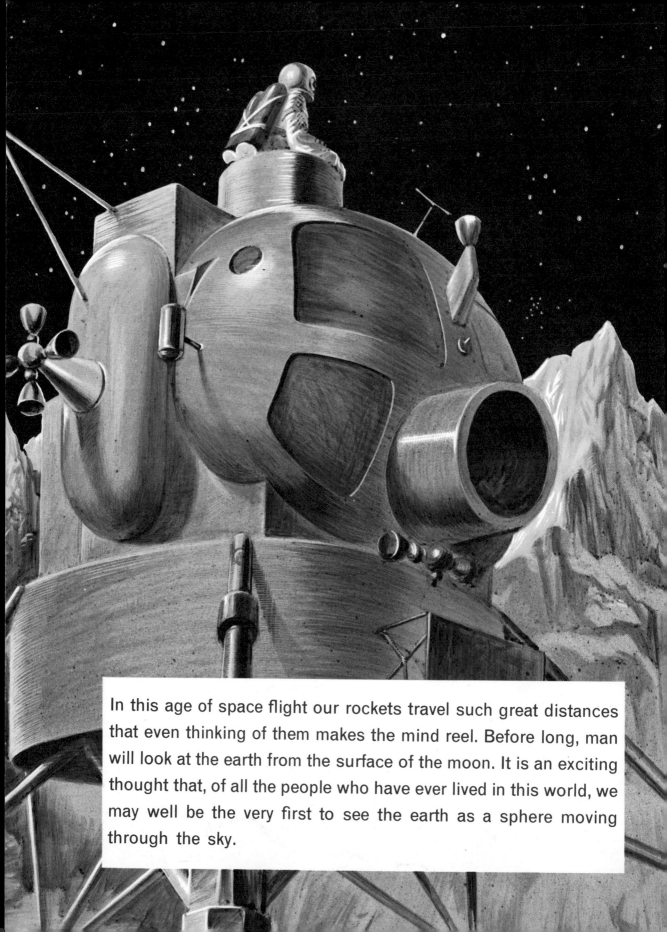

In this age of space flight our rockets travel such great distances that even thinking of them makes the mind reel. Before long, man will look at the earth from the surface of the moon. It is an exciting thought that, of all the people who have ever lived in this world, we may well be the very first to see the earth as a sphere moving through the sky.